BIG TRUTH LITTLE BOOKS®

THE DANGER OF HYPOCRISY

J.R. Cuevas

With All Wisdom Publications
Cupertino, California

THE DANGER OF HYPOCRISY

The Danger of Hypocrisy
Copyright © 2019 J.R. Cuevas
Published by WITH ALL WISDOM PUBLICATIONS
Requests for information about **BIG TRUTH** LITTLE BOOKS® can be
sent to:

Publications@creeksidebiblechurch.com

ISBN: 978-1-7336041-4-7

The Danger of Hypocrisy is volume 14 in the Big Truth little books®
series.

General Editor: Cliff McManis
Series Editor: Derek Brown
Associate Editors: J. R. Cuevas, Breanna Paniagua, Jasmine Patton
Proofreader: Sergio Gonzalez
Cover Design: Oluwasanya Awe

To my wife, Kathy
the most prudent and delightful person I know

To Mitch Douglas
a true model of integrity who pushed me to write on
this topic

CONTENTS

SERIES PREFACE

Our mission with the *BIG TRUTH little books*® series is to provide edifying, accessible literature for Christian readers from all walks of life. We understand that it is often difficult to find time to read good books. But we also understand that reading is a valuable means of spiritual growth. The answer? Get some really big truth into some little books. These books may be small, but each is full of Scripture, theological reflection, and pastoral insight. Our hope is that Christians young and old will benefit from these books as they grow in their knowledge of Christ through His Word.

Cliff McManis, General Editor
Derek Brown, Series Editor

Introduction

The Most Important Virtue and the Most Dangerous Vice

What is the over-arching quality of Christian character? It's a question that I've been pondering since college when I chose to give up my pursuit of a career in research biology for pastoral ministry. My answer to the question has changed over the years, as my perspective is much different than it was when I was first launched into ministry. Over the course of serving in multiple churches and ministry contexts while working with a men and women from various backgrounds, I've found that the answer can be distilled into a few key virtues.

That's not to say that Christian living isn't multifaceted. Perhaps that's why, during different seasons of ministry, I've found myself inadvertently emphasizing different things to the men who asked me to disciple them. To some, I would emphasize the importance of discipline and productivity. To others, I would emphasize the importance of faithfulness. Yet to others, I'd emphasize teachability as the quality to pursue. At the end of the day, all biblical virtues ought to be pursued, so that that the believer would be increasing in all things and lacking in nothing (James 1:4; 2 Pet 1:9). At the same time, there are certain character qualities that carry a heavier weight than others. As Christ said, certain commands and expectations for God's people are weightier than others (Matt 23:23). So, while Christian living and Christian character is multi-faceted, certain virtues are of higher priority than others because they affect our expression of all other virtues.

Back to the original question: What is the overarching quality of Christian character? What is the quality that authenticates and unlocks the true expression of every other virtue and every Christian endeavor? It's not a trick question. It's the virtue by which Christian *wisdom* is to be characterized according to James 3:17. It is the virtue with which *prayer* must be pursued according to Matthew 6:5. It is the virtue that must be present when one *receives the Word of God* according to 1 Peter 2:1-2 and when one *teaches the Word of God* according to 1 Timothy 4:1-3. It is the virtue that ought to be characteristic of one's *ministry and service* as described in Matthew 6:2. It is the virtue that, according to Matthew 7:5, ought to harness how we *confront the sins of others*. It is the virtue that ought to be present in our *church fellowship* as Galatians 2:13-14 teaches. It is the virtue that ought to undergird *humility and spiritual disciplines* in the Christian according to Matthew 6:16. It is the virtue that authenticates *worship* in the Christian as Christ warned in Mark 7:6-7. It is the virtue that distinguishes true *motives* from malicious *motives* according to Matthew 22:18. And before you say the answer is "love," let it be said that such a virtue is also one that ought to characterize *love* according to Romans 12:9.

It is the virtue no Christian can afford to neglect, for it unlocks the proper and acceptable expression of every other virtue, and, for that reason, just about every facet of Christian living. It is the virtue known as the biblical quality of *integrity*. With it, a Christian has everything; without it, a Christian has nothing—nothing of value in the eyes of God who searches the heart of every person. Consider the following:

- Without integrity, preaching becomes theatrics.
- Without integrity, teaching becomes brainwashing.
- Without integrity, shepherding becomes manipulation.
- Without integrity fellowship becomes socializing.
- Without integrity, wisdom becomes deception.
- Without integrity, encouragement becomes flattery.
- Without integrity, leadership becomes corruption.

- Without integrity, gentleness becomes cowardice.
- Without integrity, love becomes lust.
- Without integrity, sanctification becomes legalism.
- Without integrity, serving becomes boasting.
- Without integrity, worship becomes idolatry.
- Without integrity, Christianity becomes a cult.

But to understand integrity more deeply, one can ask a converse question: what is the most dangerous vice that a Christian can exhibit? It's a vice that is, unfortunately, present and prevalent, even in doctrinally sound, Bible-teaching churches.

Over the course of His ministry, Jesus interacted with all kinds of sinners: tax collectors, adulterers, polygamists, prostitutes, zealots, the arrogant and proud, the demon-possessed, abusive Roman soldiers, pagans, thieves, murderers, and betrayers, to name a few. From all of these groups of sinners He made converts and followers. That's the beauty of studying the Gospel of Luke in particular—watching the Son of Man seek and save even the most vile of sinners.

But there was a group of sinners with whom Jesus engaged with particular severity: the Jewish religious leaders at the time, known as the Pharisees and scribes. Jesus dealt harshly with them because they were characterized by a particular sin—a sin that not a single person in the church is immune to. Everyone is potential prey; everyone must be alert lest they fall into the condemnation of the Pharisees. It was for this particular vice that Jesus said that unless one's righteousness surpassed that of the Pharisees and scribes, one would not be able to enter into the kingdom of heaven (Matt 5:20). It is the vice that is directly antithetical to the virtue of integrity. And it was the sin that, during the week leading to His crucifixion, Jesus forthrightly, vehemently, and publicly exposed in the Pharisees and scribes.

It is the sin of hypocrisy. Hypocrisy turns preaching into theatrics.

- Hypocrisy turns teaching into brainwashing
- Hypocrisy turns shepherding into manipulation.
- Hypocrisy turns church into socializing.
- Hypocrisy turns wisdom into deception.
- Hypocrisy turns leadership into corruption.
- Hypocrisy turns gentleness into cowardice.
- Hypocrisy turns love into lust.
- Hypocrisy turns sanctification into legalism.
- Hypocrisy turns serving into boasting.
- Hypocrisy turns worship into idolatry.
- Hypocrisy turns Christianity into a cult.

For the disciple of Christ, pursuing integrity necessarily implies being wary of hypocrisy. Being wary of hypocrisy implies understanding the nature of hypocrisy. And to do so, one must turn to Christ's words about hypocrisy recorded in Matthew 23:13-33.

The Context of Matthew 23

The Gospel of Matthew, the first of the four Gospels in the New Testament, presents Jesus as the Messiah, the Anointed One to whom the Old Testament Scriptures point; the true King for whom the world has waited. And when the King of heaven came down to earth, He came not primarily to perform miracles. He came to speak. It's no wonder that when reading Matthew, one sees a side of Christ that liberal evangelicals tend to ignore—Jesus the Preacher. The book is filled with Jesus' sermons. If you want to know what it looks like to preach, listen to the Prince of Preachers Himself! Jesus preached about the King (Himself), His kingdom (the kingdom of heaven) and the people who will dwell as citizens of the kingdom (His disciples).

The sermons preached by Jesus recorded in Matthew are essentials for Christian living. Yet, the sermon that Christians seem to talk about the least is the one recorded in Matthew 23:13-33—the sermon more commonly known as "The Seven Woes." Perhaps it's because this sermon makes Christians most uncomfortable due to how it questions our own faith and integrity. In other words, if Matthew 23:13-33 describes you, then you can't have any confidence in the genuineness of your regeneration.

When Jesus preached this sermon, He was about to complete His public ministry. Having spent the majority of His three-year ministry in Galilee, He had arrived in Jerusalem on the week of Passover. He had been, from the dawning of His ministry, interacting with the religious leaders in not-so-politically-correct ways. He had meals at their homes, and shocked them with actions that went against their man-made, legalistic traditions. They had questioned Him, and He answered and explained. In several instances, they tested Him, yet He proved Himself. On numerous occasions, they tried to trap Him; each time, He escaped their traps. But on this occasion, Jesus didn't wait for them to invite Him to lunch, question Him, test Him, or attempt to trap Him. He wielded the sword of His truth and goes on the offensive. With the crowds surrounding Him, Jesus doesn't just speak about the Pharisees; He speaks *to* the Pharisees, addressing them directly. Only a few days later, the Pharisees would kill Him.

The religious leaders killed Jesus because they didn't like what He said, and they didn't like what He said because there was nothing warm and fuzzy about it. Seven times[1] Jesus addresses the Pharisees and scribes by repeatedly using the word, "Woe!" By using this word, Jesus was essentially saying, "Of all the people in the world, of all the types and categories of sinners, it is you, Pharisees and scribes, who are most liable to divine judgment." For what reason? Jesus says six times, "Woe to you, scribes and Pharisees, *hypocrites.*" Of all the words Jesus could have used to describe why

---

[1]The number of woes can be increased to eight if we include Matthew 23:14, but this verse doesn't appear in early manuscripts and likely does not belong in the text of Matthew.

God so disapproved of these religious leaders' teaching and conduct, it was the word "hypocrite" He used over and over again.

Hypocrites they were—actors, pretenders, stage-players, mask-wearers. In Jesus' time, the Greek word ὑποκριτής (*hypocrites*) was used to describe entertainers who wore masks on stage while performing dramatic stories or narratives. These actors played certain roles that were obviously inconsistent with who they really were. In its original use, a hypocrite was the ancient-day version of the Hollywood actor or Broadway performer.

I thought about this concept when my wife and I visited my younger cousin in New York to watch her perform in a Broadway musical in which she was cast. I watched her play the roles of a prostitute, soldier, and peasant villager—all in the same show. In real life, she is none of these things. The Pharisees and scribes, likewise, were not who they presented themselves to be. They had, for decades, postured themselves as the spiritual elite and the ones who truly knew God. They were the true religious leaders and the interpreters and keepers of God's law. Yet, they were spiritually bankrupt and far from God. Thus, throughout the course of His three-year ministry, Jesus rightly accused the Pharisees of hypocrisy.

Matthew, in particular, records Jesus accusing the religious leaders of hypocrisy six times (6:2, 6:5, 7:5, 15:7, and 22:18). In Matthew 23:13-33, Jesus addresses them as hypocrites six times in a single diatribe. It was the harshest and most comprehensive denunciation that Jesus ever gave in His public ministry, and it was to the group of people whom the Jews had esteemed as their religious leaders. To visualize how shocking this incident would have been, imagine Jesus walking into the sanctuary of Grace Community Church during the Shepherds Conference, stepping into the pulpit, taking the microphone, and saying to the three thousand pastors gathered from around the world, "All of you…you phonies!"

Yet, it was out of love and truth that He delivered this condemnatory sermon. He was warning the crowds of false teachers. He was shepherding His beloved sheep—for whom He was about to give His life as a ransom—away from the wolves that were trying to lure them away from the Good Shepherd and devour their faith. Because of their hypocrisy, the Pharisees and scribes were not to be followed. They were to be avoided. They were to be denounced. That is what hypocrisy deserves when Christians encounter it.

What About Us?

What does Jesus' sermon in Matthew 23 mean for us? Like all Scripture, the Gospel of Matthew was written to an original audience, but has been preserved for our instruction (Rom 15:4; 1 Cor 10:11). In this sermon is the call to the Christian to beware of hypocrisy because God hates it. Conversely, we are to pursue integrity because this is what God loves and ultimately promises to bless.

To beware of hypocrisy, we must understand it and know what it looks like. What are the marks of a hypocrite? In Matthew 23:13-33, Jesus gives us seven signs. Each of them will be identified and explained in this book. Exhibiting any one of these signs does not automatically make a person guilty of spiritual fraud. But if all seven marks appear unquestionably and consistently in an individual, then beware.

1

THE SIGNS OF HYPOCRISY, PART 1

I have a family friend who once told us the story of the day she checked herself into the hospital. She was at her home and, upon looking at the mirror in her bathroom, noticed something strange in her eyes. She immediately rushed herself to the hospital, because she knew that she was having a stroke. Sure enough, she was correct. She was experiencing a stroke, and her quick thinking enabled her to get immediate treatment (the story ends well; today, she lives as a healthy grandmother). But how did she know that she was experiencing a stroke? After all, WebMD didn't exist back then. The answer: she was a doctor. Having practiced internal medicine for nearly thirty years in multiple countries, her eyes were trained to discern the signs and symptoms of an internal cardiovascular condition whose presence would go largely unnoticed to the pedestrian eye.

Sin is first and foremost a condition of the heart. But, as Christ said, whatever is in the heart will eventually go forth from it (Matthew 15:19). A tree is known by its fruits; who a man is will show in what he does and how he lives (Matthew 7:15-20). Hypocrisy, the most deadly of spiritual diseases, cannot remain hidden. It will manifest itself and affect the entire life of a person. Its symptoms may go unnoticed to the pedestrian eye, but not to the trained eye, and definitely not to the eye of the Great Physician Himself. His eyes saw their hearts. But Christ did not simply condemn their hypocrisy privately; he confronted their hypocrisy publicly with great detail to equip and warn His disciples whom he had called to be shrewd as serpents and discern the presence of the wolves in their midst (Matthew 10:16).

As disciples of Jesus Christ, the church is called to exercise keen discernment. We are to be innocent in the purity of our character, but shrewd in our ability to discern good and evil (Hebrews 5:14). When it comes to the sin of spiritual hypocrisy, we need to know its signs and symptoms, so that we may flee from it. What, then, are the signs?

Sign #1: Hypocrites are Selfishly Competitive
Jesus begins the sermon with the first of the seven woes:

> But woe to you, scribes and Pharisees, hypocrites, because you shut off the kingdom of heaven from people; for you do

> not enter in yourselves, nor do you allow
> those who are entering to go in (Matt 23:13).

Jesus accused the religious leaders because they "shut off the kingdom of heaven" from people. Throughout their false ministries, the Pharisees and scribes had esteemed themselves as the ones who could lead people into the kingdom of heaven. They postured themselves as the ones who knew the way to God, belonged to God, and could lead others to God. Their religious chicanery was exposed in the way they treated both John the Baptist and Jesus Himself.

> For John came neither eating nor drinking,
> and they say, "He has a demon!" The Son of
> Man came eating and drinking, and they say,
> 'Behold, a gluttonous man and a drunkard, a
> friend of tax collectors and sinners (Matt
> 11:18-19)!

Jesus had designated John the Baptist as the greatest man born of women (Matt 11:11). John pointed people to Christ and the true way to heaven (John 1:29; 3:22-30). Yet the religious leaders opposed him and claimed that he was demon-possessed (Matt 11:18). It is no surprise, then, that John the Baptist exposed the Pharisees as a "brood of vipers" (Matt 3:7). They weren't born of Abraham, but of the devil! And when Christ, the King Himself, came and preached the kingdom of heaven over and over again, the Pharisees accused Him of being a glutton (Matt 11:19) and also of being demon-possessed (Matt 12:24). Such persistent rejection of both John and Jesus exposed two realities.

First, the Pharisees were unregenerate and were therefore not entering the kingdom. Second, the Pharisees and scribes did not want people to find God's kingdom. They were driven by a jealous, competitive, and self-centered spirit. Their selfishly competitive heart was exposed when someone greater than themselves came—someone who actually was selected by God to declare the truth. Their jealousy was first seen in their interaction with John the Baptist, and then with Jesus. When John and Jesus came to lead people to the kingdom, the Pharisees discredited them, defamed them, and led people away from them, thus shutting people out of the kingdom of heaven. Jesus was the door to eternal life and the kingdom of heaven (John 10:7-9). And yet, by discrediting Jesus, the Pharisees and scribes had attempted to lead people away from the entrance into heaven. Their deflection of the people away from Jesus was not due to ignorance, but due to their desire to conceal what Christ was exposing: they did not care to lead the Jews to the kingdom of heaven; they cared only about leading the people to *themselves*.

When it comes to their ambitions, hypocrites are selfishly competitive. That's not to say that all competition is bad. In fact, competition can be good. The apostle Paul affirms that all who run must run in such a way that they can win (1 Cor 9:24). It can be healthy for Christians to participate in competitive athletics, academics, and similar endeavors, because such competition promotes personal growth and skill-development. What Jesus is addressing in Matthew 23:13 is competition in the spiritual realm. When it comes to spiritual growth, ministry, and influence, Christians have no business seeking to out-compete one another. It is why the apostle Paul says to do nothing out of selfish rivalry (Phil 2:3).

Hypocrites, on the other hand, are competitive with other Christians in these realms. They are particularly competitive with those who have a similar sphere of influence. Like Diotrophes (3 John 9), they "want to be first" in people's lives. They care less about the progress and joy of people's faith (Phil 1:25) and only desire for others to "grow" if it glorifies them in the process. But as soon as someone else comes along who seems to be more gifted, more charismatic, and more capable of doing the job than they in leading those people to God, they try to compete with that person and even discredit them, be it directly or indirectly. In doing so, they lead people away from the vessel whom God may have truly sent to lead His sheep to His kingdom. They are hypocrites in the sense that they are actually leading people *away* from the place where they claim to be leading people. They are hypocrites because they pretend to care about people's spiritual growth, but in reality only care about the esteem they receive from people. They pretend to care about the glory of God, but in reality only care about their own glory.

How many times have we been guilty of this? How many times have we been in some kind of a spiritual leadership capacity during which we claimed that all we desired was the sanctity and holiness and growth of God's people, but when someone else comes along who exceeded us in talent, maturity, giftedness, and charisma and who could actually lead people to such growth and holiness, we find ourselves jealous, competing for his position, and even attempting to discredit him—however subtly—in the process. The irony of it all is that those who seek to cause others to question the integrity of a godly leader are the ones who lack integrity.

The man of integrity, on the other hand, is driven by the philosophy of John the Baptist as seen in John 3:30. As soon as Jesus arrived and began His public ministry, people began to be drawn away from John and toward Jesus. Some came to John and told him about it, only for John to respond that he himself is only the friend of the bridegroom and not the bridegroom himself. Now that Jesus had arrived, John said, "He must increase, and I must decrease" (John 3:30). Study the Scriptures, and you'll find that this was true. John the Baptist is rarely mentioned in the Gospels after Christ's baptism, and he is not mentioned at all in the epistles. The man of integrity cares not about the personal glory he can receive from leading people in the faith. All he truly cares about is that people find Christ, believe in Christ, and follow Him. He considers Christ's glory of such value and preeminence that he forgets about his own. In contrast to hypocrites, people of integrity gladly allow themselves, like John the Baptist, to decrease, if that's what is required for a more competent person to increase in his influence.

As a Christian—especially if you are a leader in the church—you must exercise extreme caution and care when you choose to discredit another person, especially one who is in a position of spiritual leadership in Christ's church. You must also be careful when endorsing another person or leader. Proverbs 20:25 says that it is rash for man to say too quickly, "It is holy." There are times when, as a pastor and elder, I have to discredit a person who may truly be a false teacher. A pastor functions as both sheepdog and livestock guarding dog. He must not only shepherd the sheep to the green pastures of the Word, but warn them when wolves are present lest he stand guilty before God (Ezek 33:7-9). But motives are of utmost importance. Discredit another believer because you are afraid that God's sheep may be led astray from a pure devotion to Christ (2 Cor 11:3). Don't discredit because you are afraid of losing your influence and preeminence in the lives of people, for that may inevitably cause you to discredit those who truly are teachers of the truth. Guard your heart from being selfishly competitive, lest you fall into hypocrisy.

Sign #2: Hypocrites are Culturally Legalistic

After accusing the Pharisees of shutting off the kingdom of heaven from people, Jesus continued the accusation by giving the second of the seven woes in the following verse.

> Woe to you, scribes and Pharisees, hypocrites, because you travel around on sea and land to make one proselyte; and when he becomes one, you make him twice as much a son of hell as yourselves (Matt 23:15)

The description is figurative; the condemnation is stunning. The Pharisees thought they were headed to heaven, but Jesus called them sons of hell. Why? Because they "traveled around on sea and land to make one proselyte." Christ speaks figuratively, in that the Pharisees and scribes were not sea voyagers by trade. What Christ was saying was that these religious leaders went to great lengths to accomplish something. They were, in fact, missions-minded people in a very real sense of the word. Christ is not condemning foreign or international missions. The apostle Paul was God's chosen vessel to the Gentiles, and he had to travel around on sea and land to make disciples of Christ in the Greco-Roman region outside of Judea and Samaria. The Pharisees had the same intensity as Paul did in their missionary efforts. But their mission was not to make disciples of Christ and worshippers of God. It was to make *proselytes*.

A proselyte was a Gentile who converted to Judaism and particularly adopted all of the traditional Jewish customs as outlined by the religious establishment, but they were not necessarily regenerate. Read enough of the Gospel accounts and compare them to the Old Testament and it won't take long to realize that the Pharisees had prescribed a number of things to the Jewish community that were never explicitly commanded by God in the Old Testament and condemned those who did not follow them. They had treated several of their man-made traditions as law to the point where they had neglected the word of God itself (Matt 15:6, Mark 7:8). What Christ was exposing about these religious leaders was their false zeal, making converts not of the truth, but of their own traditions. They were less concerned about the spiritual state of the people and more concerned with their customs and traditions being passed down. They were hypocrites in that they were pretending to convert people to be followers of God, when in reality they were wanting people to become followers of themselves and their own extra-biblical traditions. They were unashamed legalists.

Hypocrites are, by nature, culturally and traditionally legalistic. They love to promote their personal ways of doing things more than they do the principles of Scripture. They love to speak of and promote their personal disciplines, practices and convictions. They love to talk about and promote how they structure their family lives, how they raise their children, how they dated, how they structure their devotional times. While doing so, they silently condemn those who seek other ways of applying Scripture, and insist that their way is the only way. They're often intense and diligent about telling people their detailed practices of how they live out their faith and do so in an unwarranted manner or in an unsolicited way. They neglect to take into consideration that others may have different convictions and ways of doing things, failing to understand the words of Romans 14:5-6: "one person regards one day above another, another regards every day alike. Each person must be fully convinced in his own mind."

It should be no surprise, then, that hypocrites love to take the form of mentors. They love to "disciple" people, even when they are never approached for discipleship. Over the years, I've taught younger believers who are hungry for spiritual growth and discipleship to be wary of those who approach them and say, "You look like you need some discipling. How would you like it if I discipled you?" I offer this warning because hypocrites tend to be eager to be in positions of influence. And when they do disciple or mentor individuals, they have a tendency to be very intense and particular. The discipleship relationship is filled with the passing down of rules and practices more than principles. I myself have seen enough in the life of the church to know that so many of these same people who try to "pass down their wisdom" have lives that are completely disheveled. They don't need to be traveling around land and sea mentoring people; what they need is help getting their lives together! Yet, they don't, because they're not truly concerned about spiritual growth or Christ. They're concerned about culture and tradition. It's no wonder that such people, though they claim to be transformed by the truth, tend to only spend time with people who are just like them—be it ethnically, socio-economically, or traditionally.

Over the last few years, my wife and I have spent a substantial amount of time watching documentaries on different cults. Though these cults are unrelated and express their false religion differently, they each share some common key features. One of the features that usually exist within a cult a culture of uniformity on just about everything, including what people eat, how they dress, where they live, how they talk, how they approach their children's education and discipline, and much more.

Uniformity to such a degree issues a red flag, because God's church was not designed to have uniformity across every facet of Christian living. Uniformity is different from unity and harmony. Unity and harmony are to be pursued amongst God's people (Phil 2:1-2). But with unity, there also ought to exist diversity in the manner with which different Christians carry out the same biblical principles. The apostle Paul states:

One person regards one day above another, another regards every day alike. Each person must be fully convinced in his own mind. He who observes the day, observes it for the Lord, and he who eats, does so for the Lord, for he gives thanks to God; and he who eats not, for the Lord he does not eat, and gives thanks to God (Rom 14:5-6).

The reality of Christ's lordship over believers will be expressed in a variety of forms, even within the same local body. This applies to eating, drinking, observing particular days over others, children's education, views on television and social media, and family devotions, to name a few. Genuine discipleship allows for the presence of such differences among God's people without sacrificing the principle of Christ's lordship (Rom 14:7-8). Hypocrites, however, go beyond this principle and insist on their detailed practices. They say: "I home-school, and so should you. I fast one Monday a month, and so should you. I pray submerged in the swimming pool for 3 minutes every morning, and so should you. I abstain from all forms of television, and so should you."

In contrast, men of integrity don't go around trying to make disciples of themselves. They don't go around land and sea trying to promote themselves. Rather, their lives speak for themselves, and people imitate them because they witness the outcome of their lives (Heb 13:7). Such people don't really care if anyone else in the church desires to imitate them directly, as long as they know that those people are living for the Lord.

On a higher level, churches that are marked by integrity are churches that don't try to shove a lifestyle down people's throats. They don't force people to be on a particular Bible reading plan. They don't guilt-trip their married couples into going on weekly date nights (even though they can be very helpful! But that is for another book). They don't guilt the families in the church into thinking that sending their kids to public school is akin to selling their souls to Satan. They don't promote a uniform standard of living. They don't pretend to teach the Bible when they're in fact teaching culture. They are, instead, primarily concerned with how their members are relating to Christ Himself, for He Himself is the one Leader of His people (Matt 23:10).

One of the most significant, and difficult, lessons that I've learned when it comes to shepherding God's flock is that the more authority is vested in me, the less freedom I actually have to share my opinions on certain matters of life. It sounds counterintuitive, but it is a biblical reality nevertheless. The reason is due to the title I carry. The title of "pastor" connotes the presence of authority. And with authority comes weight of opinion on the shoulders of those under your care. I've come to realize that my opinions carry more weight than they would had I not been a pastor—for the better or for the worse. If I am not careful, what I intend to be an opinion could be taken as law or even wisdom, and it is much harder for Christians to shake off opinions of their pastors than it is fellow church members, even if they themselves don't agree with those opinions.

As a father, for instance, I certainly have my preferences about which educational system would be best for our children among the choices of public schooling, home-schooling, private secular schooling, or private Christian schooling (We have tried three of these four with our son). I realize, however, that I have to be careful in sharing my opinion to fellow fathers in our congregation. It may be that God is leading him to send his children to a different system than I have chosen to send mine, yet because of my position he may feel pressured to do the same as me. Because of my pastoral position, members regularly ask for my opinion about everything—whether they should buy a bigger house, what I think about their girlfriend as a potential spouse, whether or not I think they should move to this or that state, whether they should pursue a graduate degree, whether they should leave and find another church, what Bible reading plan they should be on, whether they should allow their children to spend time with non-believing classmates, and many more. I have learned to be cautious so that I don't end up making a proselyte instead of a disciple of Christ. For true men of integrity seek not to make personal proselytes, but disciples of Christ.

Sign #3: Hypocrites are Morally Inconsistent

Continuing His condemnation of the Pharisees and scribes, Christ described their hypocrisy seen in their moral inconsistency in Matthew 23:16-21:

> Woe to you, blind guides, who say, "Whoever swears by the temple, that is nothing; but whoever swears by the gold of the temple is obligated." You fools and blind men! Which is more important, the gold or the temple that sanctified the gold? And, "Whoever swears by the altar, that is nothing, but whoever swears by the offering on it, he is obligated." You blind men, which is more important, the offering, or the altar that sanctifies the offering? Therefore, whoever swears by the altar, swears both by the altar and by everything on it. And whoever swears by the temple, swears both by the temple and by Him who dwells within it. And whoever swears by heaven, swears both by the throne of God and by Him who sits upon it.

In exposing their hypocrisy, Christ specifically exposes the error of the scribes and Pharisees teaching about swearing by the temple. With regard to swearing and making oaths, the religious leaders had taught that their obligations to fulfill the requirements of their oaths was dependent upon whether or not they appealed to the gold of the temple in the making of the oath. In the same way, they taught that the one who swore by the altar was not obligated to fulfill that oath if there was no sacrifice present on the altar at the time of the oath; they were only required to fulfill their oath if there was a sacrifice present. The religious leaders were making distinctions between swearing in different settings and circumstances, claiming that it was acceptable to swear yet not fulfill an oath in some instances and not others, based on a superficial set of criteria. In effect, they were promoting compartmentalization and inconsistency. They focused not on the integrity of their character but on behaving differently depending on what suited them best and basing their decision on shallow reasons.

Such conduct is akin to the man who says, "It's fine to curse when I'm around my non-Christian friends, but not in front of my Christian friends" or "it's acceptable to lie when I'm at work, so long as I don't do it at church." The Pharisees, in implementing these loopholes into their oath making, were trying to justify lying and morally inconsistent behavior. Christ, therefore, calling them blind, twice interrogates them with rhetorical questions and then declares: "Whoever swears by the temple, swears both by the temple and by Him who dwells within it. And whoever swears by heaven, swears by both the throne of God and by Him who sits upon it" (Matt 23:21-22). In other words, God is present both in the temple and in the throne of heaven. Thus, if you swear by the temple, you are swearing by God. And when you swear by heaven, you are swearing by God. Either way, God is present to hear your oath. What difference does it make then, Christ asks, that you made your oath before the temple or the altar or by heaven? Regardless of the circumstances, God was there.

So, for the high school kid who has a Clorox-wiped mouth in church and a potty-mouth at school: he ought to remember that he speaks before God who is present with him both at the Wednesday school hour and at Sunday church service. The Pharisees would have argued otherwise because they were characterized by moral inconsistency—pretending to be one way in one setting but behaving another way in a different setting.

To be clear, I am not advocating uniform behavior in every set of circumstances. Proverbs 27:14 wisely instructs timeliness for certain exhibitions of behavior: "He who blesses his friend with a loud voice early in the morning, It will be reckoned a curse to him." Different events do, at times, call for different codes of conduct. You can cheer when you're with your kids at a baseball game, but you probably shouldn't cheer during your grandmother's funeral.

What I am emphasizing here is the *moral* portrait of a man. Hypocrites are morally inconsistent by nature. They are compartmentalizers, behaving according to one set of moral criteria when they're at home and another one when they're with the church family, and yet under another one when they're with their coworkers at work. It's for this reason that I've learned, when trying to inquire of the spiritual condition of an individual, to not ask the question "How are you doing spiritually?" It's not necessarily a bad question. But if you want to know how people are doing spiritually, the better thing to do is to ask them about every other area of life. Ask them about their marriage. Ask them about their relationship with their children. Ask them how things have been going at work and how they've been submitting (or not submitting) to their boss. Look at their financial budget and how they spend their money. Inquire about their relationship with their parents. Ask them to list out how they spend their free time. And then ask yourself, "Are you seeing the same person *morally* in all of these areas?" A hypocrite, because he is morally inconsistent, will not. They will make superficial distinctions and demarcations rather than focusing on the consistency of his or her character. They are experts in crafting double, triple, and quadruple standards. They're akin to chameleons, changing the color of their conduct depending on the people they are around. They are hypocrites because they pretend to be one person in one setting and another person in another setting.

I remember interviewing a young man who had wanted to become a member the church where I was serving at the time. He told us why he had wanted to become a member and professed his faith in Jesus Christ. By all external and observable accounts from our end, he was a decent Christian man. But he was unaware that previous to the interview, we had been informed by one of his friends that this prospective member habitually went to parties with his non-Christian friends and got drunk in the process. He thought he could behave one way with his Christian friends and another way with his non-Christian ones. His Christian friends confronted him about it, but he would brush it off and turn a deaf ear, so his friends came and communicated this information to the pastoral staff. We confronted him on the issue, and he admitted to the inconsistency. We denied him membership, and counseled him to address his spiritual life. He never did return, and I don't know where he is currently in his relationship with God or if he even has one at all.

Men of integrity, on the other hand, do what they do with the cognizance that the God who the heavens and the earth cannot contain is everywhere, all the time, and always in their presence. No matter where they are they don't change their principles of conduct, because they understand that God does not change in what He expects from them. They realize that wherever they are, they are called to the same standard of holiness (1 Pet 1:15-16). It is for integrity's sake that 1 Timothy 3:7 demands that the man who serves as an elder have a good reputation outside of the church, for a man who behaves one way outside of the church and another way inside of the church has no business being behind the pulpit preaching the Word of God that he so inconsistently heeds. Men of integrity are those who carry the same moral reputation amongst all spheres of relationships. They are men who, contrary to hypocrites, are morally consistent.

Are you the same person on and off the court? Do you exhibit the same level of morality and standard of ethic regardless of who you are around? If I were to ask five different people who interact with you from five different relational spheres (i.e. home, church, work, athletics, extended family) to describe the kind of person you are, would they all paint the same portrait?

Yet, five people giving a consistent testimony about you doesn't exonerate you. Spiritual morality is more than just being consistent. You can be consistently wrong. Further, being a staunch ecumenist (the opposite of being competitive), a flaming antinomian (the opposite of being legalistic), and morally rigid (the opposite of being morally inconsistent) does not equate to being a person of integrity. Needless to say, Jesus does not stop after identifying the first three. He identifies four more, all of which are discussed in the next chapter.

2

THE SIGNS OF HYPOCRISY, PART 2

One of the reasons why hypocrisy can go unnoticed to the untrained eye is because those who practice it are not always overtly malicious, violent, or belligerent people. County sheriffs aren't commissioned to look for hypocrites. It would be unfitting for a judge to sentence someone to prison because "they showed signs of hypocrisy." Hence, it must have felt like an electric shock to the both the onlookers and the religious leaders themselves when Jesus publicly denounced their character and warned His disciples to beware of them. But if they weren't breaking into homes, sleeping with multiple women, murdering the innocent, or selling drugs, what were they doing that warranted such condemnation? If hypocrites pose no physical threat to society, how can you identify them? How do you identify a most dangerous of vices when those who exhibit it don't seem to be outwardly hurting anyone?

Thankfully, our Good Shepherd has not left His sheep alone to craft our own list of signs and symptoms. Picking up from where we left off in chapter 1, we will now consider four more signs of hypocrisy.

Sign #4: Hypocrites are Morally Disproportionate

As He continues to address the morality of the Pharisees and scribes, Jesus unveils another facet of their hypocrisy in Matthew 23:23-24:

> Woe to you, scribes and Pharisees, hypocrites! For you tithe mint and dill and cumin, and have neglected the weightier provisions of the law: justice and mercy and faithfulness; but these are the things you should have done without neglecting the others. You blind guides, who strain out a gnat and swallow a camel!

The Pharisees were traditionalist tithers, and they were fastidious about their traditions. Christ exposes their particular way of tithing, "you tithe mint and dill and cumin." As a practice, the Pharisees would take every tenth strand of the mint and dill leaves, (already very thin), separate them out and give them to the offering. It was a method of tithing that was incredibly meticulous, arduous, and disciplined. It was also non-mandatory. God never commanded the tithing of mint, dill, and cumin in the Old Testament Law.

There is nothing wrong with doing something for the Lord that isn't mandated Scripture and that Scripture doesn't condemn. There are plenty of practices today that are part of Christians' regular disciplines that Scripture doesn't prescribe but that can be helpful nevertheless. Journaling, reading ten chapters of the Bible a day, fasting, or going on prayer walks around the lake are but a few examples that some Christians have found useful. The Pharisees were not hypocrites because they tithed mint and dill and cumin. They were hypocrites because of their twisted motives and the disproportion that characterized their spirituality as a whole. The Pharisees wanted to make it seem as if they were going above and beyond what was required of them in the area of giving, mostly to show off. And this motive was revealed in their neglect of the weightier matters of the Law.

This is the condemnation: they were diligent and above-and-beyond with their tithing, but neglected the heavier priorities of the Law, the priorities that would not come to an end even after Christ's sacrifice was completed: the exercising of justice, mercy, and faith (see Mic 6:8). The Pharisees were fastidious about tithing, but they neglected the proper treatment of people. They were so concerned about their own traditions that they neglected caring for people's needs.

We see this disproportionate concern for their traditions when Jesus healed the man with the withered hand (Mark 3:1-6) and the woman with a bent back (Luke 13:10-17). On both occasions, the Pharisees asked whether or not it was lawful to heal on the Sabbath. Nowhere in the Old Testament did God say that one could not tend to sick people on the Sabbath. Christ points out that domestic livestock that fell into a well on the Sabbath day were to be helped out of the pit (Matt 12:11; Luke 14:5) and even an ox or donkey that was parched on the Sabbath was to be given water (Luke 13:15).

I personally remember one particular instance when, because of a very tragic event that had occurred in my family's life, I requested a month off from my pastoral duties to heal. On one particular Sunday evening during that month, I decided to attend a church event. After the event ended, I found myself in a conversation with one of the young men who I was discipling. What was supposed to be a small talk conversation quickly turned into a counseling conversation in which he began to share some of the problems he was struggling with. I stopped him in the middle of it and said, "John, you do realize that I'm on time off, right?" He responded, "If one of your cattle falls into the well on the Sabbath, aren't you supposed to help him back out?!" Humorous as it was, it was a sharp reminder that the needs of people are more important than the extra-biblical policies I set for myself, regardless of how helpful I may find them to be. The Pharisees did not get this. They were pretending to be over-and-above in their obedience to the Law, when in fact they were being wholly disobedient to the most crucial parts of the Law.

Hypocrites carry out their lives disproportionately. They are imbalanced at best and are not comprehensive regarding which parts of the Bible they read and apply. They love to correct others on secondary gray matters yet they neglect to actually love God and love people. Such is the man who loves to wear a suit and tie to church every Sunday because he wants to "Give God his best" and yet is willing to be untruthful about his taxes and fibs on his time clock at work—pretending to give glory to God in sporting attire that the Bible doesn't prescribe, and yet disobeying God's command to be truthful and have just balances (Prov 11:1). Such hypocrites are those who attend every Sunday school class, every fellowship meal, every church event in order to make themselves appear to be devout Christians and at the same time fail to care for their aging parents while continuing to provoke their children to anger. This is the man who likes to debate the finer points of eschatology with theologians yet neglects to provide for his household. These are the people who are hyper-critical in their disapproval of electric guitars and drums played during the church worship service and yet fail to ever ask anyone around them how they are doing and never pray for their leaders.

The prevalence of such lopsided behavior is a tragic reality. Quite frankly, there are a lot of things about church life that are so meticulously discussed that have little value in the larger picture of God's global redemptive work. Whether or not the church sanctuary has blue or brown carpet does not matter. Whether we sing hymns or contemporary worship songs is a matter of preference, not doctrine. Whether the pastor should dress in a suit or tie doesn't matter (and changes anyway, depending on where he's preaching geographically). Whether Sunday service starts at 8:00 am or 11:00 am should make no difference for God's people. Whether the pastor preaches from the NASB Bible or the ESV Bible can make a difference but should not be a matter of debate or division. The type of food served in the post-service church lunch should not be a matter of great debate or importance. Whether or not, as a Christian, you drink coffee or abstain from soda is of little value in the kingdom of God. Whether or not we split Sunday school classes by age brackets or life-season demographics should not be a hill to die on.

Matters that are not explicitly addressed in Scripture should be given less weight than ones that are. What matters is that the Word is preached and the ministry of the gospel is furthered to the ends the earth. What matters is that the saints of God are worshipping in the Spirit and glory of Christ Jesus. What matters is that once immature Christians are growing in their maturity and active in their ministry. What matters is that the Christian marriages in the church reflect Christ's relationship with His church. What matters is that the saints are filled with moral purity and continually call upon the name of the Lord in prayer. Hypocrites, by nature, love to make mountains out of molehills and yet fail to rescue the sheep stuck at the edge of the cliff!

Another example of such moral disproportion can be seen in the realm of speech. I was once asked by a young believer who was jaded by the church environment in which he grew up why it is that Christians believe that cussing is wrong. It was an interesting question, because the young man who asked me the question was not someone who cussed. But before I was able to give an answer, he explained that his confusion arose from the fact that the same Christians who condemn cussing are also those who gossip. It was a fair inquiry, and an insightful one. It is true that cussing is wrong, and should never be practiced in the community of God's people (Eph 4:29). But when it comes to speech, the Bible condemns gossip as well. And not only that, but the Bible speaks far more about gossip than it does about cussing. Moreover, gossip is far more destructive to relationships and the reputation of individuals than cussing. For instance, though I would prefer neither to happen, I would much rather be a victim of someone who cussed at me out of anger than someone who gossiped about me to others out of bitterness. I've been the victim of both, and I can attest that the gossip was by far more destructive to my ministry and my relationships than the cuss words that were hurled at me. To condemn cussing while engaging in gossip is exhibiting moral disproportion, which is hypocrisy. This is but an example of so many other ways we exhibit moral disproportion.

People of integrity, on the other hand, are more concerned about the weightier matters of the law. They are more concerned with the spiritual health of people than the smoothness of the church programs. They are more concerned about doing what is right than doing what is popular. They are more concerned about being faithful than about being flashy. They are just people; they always do what they know to be right. They are merciful people; they genuinely care about the needs of others. They are faithful people; they seek to please God in all aspects of their lives. A person of integrity is a person of priority. He or she is not dogmatic about things that aren't explicitly stated in the Bible, but is unwavering in the things that are.

Sign #5: Hypocrites are Wrongly Motivated

It feels almost as if Christ's voice is getting louder by the line. As He continues to expose the hypocrisy of the Pharisees, He rebukes them for their ulterior motives in 23:25-26:

> Woe to you, scribes and Pharisees, hypocrites! For you clean the outside of the cup and of the dish, but inside they are full of robbery and self-indulgence. You blind Pharisee, first clean the inside of the cup and of the dish, so that the outside of it may become clean also.

The Pharisees and scribes were fastidious not only in their tithing practices but also in their cleansing rituals. Again, so many of the practices that they prescribed to the people of God were extra-biblical. That included all that they did regarding cleansing rituals. While there was physical cleansing prescribed in the Old Testament, particularly in the book of Leviticus, the religious leaders of Jesus' time took it to another level in their cleansing of cups and dishes. Jesus uses this as an illustration of their corrupt motives. He says that they were those who "clean the outside of the cup and of the dish" but inside they are "full of robbery and self-indulgence."

The Pharisees and scribes were those who were focused on their external appearance rather than their internal state. They loved fasting and publicly praying and making people aware of it (Matt 6:1-5). But while they were disciplined in practicing their cleansing rituals, they also took advantage of people and robbed the homes of widows. They didn't care for people, but rather used people for their own gain. They tithed with mint and dill, but internally they were lovers of money. They pretended to be pious on the outside but they were corrupt on the inside. They were those fleeced people for selfish gain, all in the name of holiness. It was no surprise then that, on two separate occasions, Jesus entered the temple and cleansed it, saying that the people had turned what was meant to be a house of prayer into a den of robbers (John 2:13-22; Luke 19:45-46). It can be assumed that the Pharisees and scribes, the keepers of the Law and managers of the temple, spear-headed such corruption.

One of the most important questions I was ever asked in a pastoral candidacy interview was the following: "What would you do if you saw the senior pastor taking money from the church offering plate?" I gave the obvious answer: "Of course I would call him out." In my head, I remember thinking, "What Christian would ever do such a thing?" Sadly, years later, I realize that things of this nature actually happen, and they do so more often than I would have expected. That question wasn't asked for the sake of hypothetical theory, but from previous experience. Corruption exists. It exists in the world, and it exists in the church.

Hypocrites are wrongly motivated. They care more about how they come across to other than what God sees when no one is looking. They are obsessed with how others think of them, to the extent that they spend large amounts of time "cleaning the outside of the cup" but not the inside of the cup. They are master-manipulators with hidden agendas, pretending to have a deep concerned for the things of God and the needs of people but in the end are motivated by selfish gain at the expense of others' welfare. Some even make a living off of taking advantage of people. Their speech—the outside of the cup—is smooth; they work on their charisma. Yet, they don't care about anyone else but themselves. But the truth inevitably comes out over time.

In the course of my life I have spoken to victims of youth workers who used their position of spiritual leadership to sexually molest them. I have interacted with ministers whom I would later find out were using their positions as counselors as an opportunity for adultery, taking advantage of the emotionally fragile women they were counseling. I have known men who used their leadership positions to steal money from the institution where they worked.

One cannot emphasize enough the danger of worldly lusts and greed that can lead one into a life of hypocrisy. This means, then, that one cannot emphasize *motives* enough. Motives, in a way, are everything. Sinful motives always make the cup unclean, no matter how much dish soap you use to clean the outside.

I recall a conversation I once had with a man whom I had commended for always spending time with the "lowly" people of the church—those who others found difficult to spend time with. I admired him for what I thought I had observed as humility of mind. But the day came years later when he admitted to me that one of the main reasons why he spent time with those people was because he was insecure; he surrounded himself with these "lowly" people as a way to make himself look good before others. He admitted that he had been taking advantage of the socially awkward in order to bring attention to himself. He was, paradoxically, honest about his hypocrisy.

People of integrity, on the other hand, refuse to take advantage of people. They have no hidden agendas; what you see is what you get. They refuse to take what belongs to others to make it theirs. They simply do what they do because they care, never asking the question "What can I get out of this person?" but instead always asking, "What can I give to this person, even if it costs me something?" As they understand that Christ gave up His life for them, so also they give up their lives for others and seek no gain in the process, truly loving with deed and truth (1 John 3:16-18).

Sign #6: Hypocrites are Pretentiously Unwholesome

Just when one thought Christ's diatribe could not become harsher, it does. When He arrives at His words in Matthew 23:27-28, Christ switches from exposing what the Pharisees and scribes *were doing* to now exposing who they *were*. He gives the following denunciation:

> Woe to you, scribes and Pharisees, hypocrites! For you are like whitewashed tombs which on the outside appear beautiful, but inside they are full of dead men's bones and all uncleanness. So you, too, outwardly appear righteous to men, but inwardly you are full of hypocrisy and lawlessness.

In first-century Jerusalem, there were no memorial parks with underground tombs and epitaphs like we see today. Tombs were used to encase Israeli people's dead bodies, but these tombs were usually above ground, so tomb-keepers took great pains to decorate and burnish the exterior of these tombs. They washed them and kept them pure looking from the outside. Thus, all foreigners visiting Jerusalem would have been impressed by the appearance of the tombs. They were well-presented, and well constructed. Indeed, it would have been quite painstaking to maintain these tombs. But a tomb-keeper, for all his effort and labor, was only called to take care of the external part of the tomb. No efforts were made to care for the inside of the tomb. It would have been unclean to do so. Thus, these white-washed tombs were beautiful structures on the outside but filled with rotting flesh and deteriorating bones in the inside.

It would have been the ultimate insult to compare someone to a whitewashed tomb, but this is just what Jesus did with the religious leaders. Jesus was condemning their hypocrisy in light of their pretentious, unwholesome nature. Previously in Matthew's gospel Christ taught that it is those who are pure in heart who are blessed, for they will see God (Matt 5:8). For the Pharisees, there was an incongruity between their external appearance and their internal motives, and that is the contrast Christ is making here. The Pharisees were interested in appearing righteous, but they were not actually hungry and thirsty for righteousness. They were interested in being seen as spiritually honorable. In reality, they were spiritually unregenerate. They wanted recognition, not righteousness.

There was a doctor who once told a story of a man in his mid-twenties who was admitted into the hospital and close to death. He was chiseled, muscular, and in appeared to be in terrific shape. Given his physical condition, he should have been running routes and dodging tackles on the football field or hiking up Everest. Yet there he was, on the hospital bed. The reason was that he had taken so many steroids to amplify his outward appearance that he had damaged his internal organs—particularly his liver. And he's not alone. There are, according to this same doctor, many young men today in their mid-twenties and thirties who are dying because of heart disease linked to steroid use which they used to make themselves look more muscular.

At the same time, you might find many senior citizens north of sixty who are still playing sports and running marathons. They don't look physically impressive because they spend a lot less time worrying about their external physique and more time worrying about the internal physical condition.

Hypocrites, like the man dying from steroid use, exhibit an incongruity between what people see on the outside and what is actually happening on the inside. Who we see is not who they are! I remember a woman who would regularly flatter my wife to her face. We later found out that she was gossiping about my wife behind her back. She exhibited this sign of hypocrisy, with her external words not matching up with her internal motives. Likewise, are men who love to kiss and hug their wives and kids in public but humiliate them in private. These are the men who praise God lavishly in public, but rarely if ever pray to Him in private. They sing songs loudly during the worship hour, but really don't find God beautiful or glorious in their hearts. In fact, they rarely ever think about God. These are the men who preach themselves as examples of purity to younger people, yet are living lives of immorality without repentance in private. As Christ said, they are those who "honor Me with their lips, but their hearts are far from Me. In vain, they worship Me" (Mark 7:6-7).

The reason why such people are like this is because, as hypocrites, they're obsessed with the external. They're obsessed with titles and accomplishments (Matt 23:7). They're obsessed with saving face and primarily concerned about their public reputation than they are about the internal condition of their heart and soul. It's for this reason that they pray long and fancy prayers in front of people, but rarely ever pray when no one is looking. It's for this reason that such people love to carry around large study Bibles when they show up in church, and yet almost never read it. They'll fake an appearance in order for people to think a certain way about them that is disingenuous.

One of the most commonly used platforms today for hypocrites is social media. Browse your Facebook newsfeed, and you'll see about five hundred pictures of people engaging in their fancies with captions like the following: "My wonderful husband wanted to show me how special I was...so he took me to this fancy restaurant on the top of Mount Denali on a Palomino Arabian Stallion." Recent studies have shown, however, that a majority of the people who post such things for the public to see are, in reality, living in troubled households. Out of insecurity of what others may think, they post the things that they do in order to get people to think that all is going well, when in reality things are not going well. They don't realize it, but they're washing the outside of their tombs.

What is difficult about this particular brand of hypocrisy is that such a vice is actually taught in various cultures. I speak personally from my own upbringing. I grew up in a culture where saving face was not seen as a vice, but a necessity. There's a particular term for it used in the native language of my country, and I hear it used frequently amongst the older generation. Saving face is considered more important than getting help when you need it. When I married my wife, I found out that the culture in which she was raised was similar in this regard. And such a reality is seen in almost every culture. In fact, I once spoke with an American-based immigrant from Asia who told me that one of the reasons why people from her culture almost never go to counseling (even if they are in desperate need of it) is because they are so afraid of people thinking they struggle that they would rather continue to struggle and save face than to be transparent about their struggles and actually get some help in the process.

Pretentious hypocrisy is not only wicked to the core; it is also dangerous. As a youth pastor and as a school teacher, I have never observed kids who were more angry at their parents than those who felt like their parents were hypocrites, and hypocrites of the kind described above. Never have I seen angrier young people than the ones who see an incongruity between who their parents present themselves to be and who their parents say they are. I've sat in front of teenage boys venting about their parents' hypocrisy so furiously they weren't able to stop crying and yelling at the same time.

Whenever youth accuse their parents of this kind of pretense, I become worried. I don't draw conclusions, as every case must be given its proper weight and witness, but I grow concerned nevertheless.

It doesn't matter how nice things look on the outside. I grow worried because there is a high chance that the child will begin to behave dangerously—either toward himself, his parents, or both. It is near impossible to grow up in an atmosphere of whitewashed tombs—beautiful on the outside but filled with rotten corpses on the inside—and not react with violence of some sort.

People of integrity, on the other hand, are consistent. They're not perfect, but they are virtuous on the inside. Who they are on the outside is a reflection of who they are on the inside. They are those who praise God lavishly in public and weep before Him in private. These are the men and women who sing songs loudly during the worship hour, but also love to read their Bible at home in private in order to gaze upon the beauty of the Lord. These are the saints whose secret and private devotional matches their public worship life (Matt 6:5-6).

These are the men and women who will not flatter in public but then slander in private; instead, as faithful friends, they will confront and rebuke their friend in private and affirm him before others in public. People of integrity are not primarily concerned about appearance. What they do care about is the part of them that others don't see. Why? Because they're primarily concerned about pleasing the God who they cannot see! They remember God's words to Samuel in 1 Samuel 16:7: "God *sees* not as man sees, for man looks at the outward appearance, but the LORD looks at the heart.

Because of this, such people are not afraid to admit when they are wrong and they are honest about when they have fallen short. What you see is indeed what you will get. They say what they mean and they mean what they say. These are the men who don't force their kids to pretend to love Jesus in front of people. They know that the way to the cross is not to put on a costume of righteousness, but to approach the Lord in humble contrition, understanding that Christ died because they were filthy, not because they were beautiful.

Sign #7: Hypocrites are Self-Righteous

The very last of the seven woes is by no means the least significant. Christ, in His final accusation that would be prophetic of what the religious leaders would indeed do to Him a few days later, states in 23:29-31:

> Woe to you, scribes and Pharisees, hypocrites! For you build the tombs of the prophets and adorn the monuments of the righteous, and say, 'If we had been living in the days of our fathers, we would not have been partners with them in shedding the blood of the prophets.' So you testify against yourselves, that you are sons of those who murdered the prophets.

The first century Jews were masters of the Old Testament, particularly the Pharisees and scribes. They had known that righteous prophets like Isaiah and others were persecuted and killed, not by pagans, but by their very own countrymen. Thus, the religious leaders of Christ's time would build tombs for the prophets to honor them as the great men of Jewish history, as if the religious leaders themselves were true men of God. They self-righteously claimed that they would have treated these Old Testament prophets better than their forefathers and ancestors did who put to death God's mouthpieces. They claimed that they wouldn't have acted as ignorantly, and yet, they proved themselves even worse than those who murdered the prophets. In just a few days, they would murder the Son of God Himself, who came not just as a mouthpiece of God, but as God Himself, the exact representation of God's nature. They pretended to be more righteous than the idolatry-plagued Israelites of the old, when they were actually worse. True hypocrites they were.

Hypocrites are by nature self-righteous. Quite simply, they see themselves as better than others. Though they may not verbally admit it, they believe that they are above falling into the sins that trap others. When they read the Scriptures, they read to control others and not themselves (see Rom 2:21). I cannot tell you how many times I've had someone, upon completing some sermon, come up to me and say, "Pastor, that was great. I know someone who really needed to hear that!" They don't see themselves as the ones needing the healing of the Great Physician. They don't see themselves as the wretched sinners who need the sanctifying work of the Spirit in their lives. They are those who look at others in sin and say, "I'm above that; I would never fall into that kind of wickedness." It's no wonder that such people are those who are experts at pointing out specs in the eyes of others when they have the entire Sequoia Redwood Forest growing in theirs!

As Christians we need to exhibit great caution in how we respond to others' sins. To be clear, certain sins have more destructive consequences than others. Committing murder has more severe consequences than losing one's temper; committing adultery results in far more pain toward one's spouse than viewing pornography. And to be sure, Christ does call us to render a verdict on the sins of others and commands the church to administer discipline on those who refuse to repent. Abstaining from self-righteousness does not mean that we tolerate sin in the church.

But as Christians, when upon hearing about the sins that others have committed—regardless of the degree of the sin—we ought never to react with an attitude of arrogance. There's a difference in saying, "May I never commit this sin" versus saying in your heart, "There's no way I can ever fall into this sin." The former is the right attitude; the latter is a dangerous one. The apostle Paul warns of this in 1 Corinthians 10:12: "Therefore let him who thinks he stands take heed that he does not fall." In other words, the Christian who thinks that he will not fall into the sins he sees others commit ought to watch himself, lest he himself fall into those same sins. In Galatians 6:1, Paul instructs: "Brethren, even if anyone is caught in any trespass, you who are spiritual, restore such a one in a spirit of gentleness; *each one* looking to yourself, so that you too will not be tempted." Whenever we deal with others who have sinned, no matter how grievous the sin, we ought to have one eye on ourselves as well lest we fall into temptation of the same sin.

As one who did not grow up in an evangelical Christian household and who didn't give his life to Christ until college, I have spent more than half of my life integrated in non-Christian communities in the Philippines, Hawaii, Los Angeles, as Las Vegas. People are often amused at the fact that I spent my high school years in Las Vegas, which is more notoriously known as "Sin City." Thus, in my life as a non-Christian and living in the non-Christian community, I have seen all of the deeds of the flesh manifested—fornication, adultery, theft, domestic violence, suicide, child molestation, abandoning of families, child pornography, homosexuality amongst both men and women, perjury, drunkenness, and drug abuse, to name a few.

What many are surprised to hear is that, now as a minister in the Christian community, I have seen every single one of these sins committed in the church. If I were to make a list of all the sins I've witnessed in the non-Christian community and make a second list of all the sins I've witnessed in the church, the list would look virtually identical. That Christians are progressively sanctified does not mean that our susceptibility to sin has decreased over the course of our lives. If anything, we ought to be more alert because the more we grow in Christ, the more we become targeted by Satan who prowls around like a roaring lion waiting for someone to devour (1 Pet 5:8). In fact, something else that I have observed in the church is at times the people who are harshest in their condemnation of others for the sins they commit over time are the ones committing the same kind of sins. It's tragic, but true.

People of integrity, on the other hand, understand in their hearts not only that they are sinners but that they are the *chief of sinners*. They understand that it was their sin that put Christ on the cross. They understand that it was their sin that was forgiven through Christ's substitutionary atonement. People of integrity don't see themselves as above sin or temptation that they observe in others, and therefore do everything they can to steer clear of it (1 Cor 10:12). These are the people who listen to sermons, and the first thought in their minds is, "I need to make some changes" and they immediately get to work and ask for accountability.

Beware, then, of the danger of thinking that you are above the sins of others. Don't ever assume yourself to be a racehorse in a stable full of donkeys, or an eagle in a roost of chickens

3

THE EFFECTS OF
HYPOCRISY

A life filled with hypocrisy is a life that counts as nothing before God. That is the fruit of hypocrisy. As I mentioned earlier, integrity is the virtue with which every other Christian virtue must be substantiated. While the previous chapters spoke of the signs of hypocrisy, one must also understand the overall effect of unchecked hypocrisy in one's life.

Where Hypocrisy is Present,
Heavenly Wisdom is Absent

Every Christian is called to acquire biblical wisdom. The book of Proverbs states that the one who finds wisdom finds life (Prov 8:35). However, there is a difference between earthly wisdom from below and heavenly wisdom from above. Earthly wisdom will lead one to destruction, while heavenly wisdom leads to blessing. James 3:13-17 describes the distinction:

> Who among you is wise and understanding? Let him show by his good behavior his deeds in the gentleness of wisdom. But if you have bitter jealousy and selfish ambition in your heart, do not be arrogant and *so* lie against the truth. This wisdom is not that which comes down from above, but is earthly, natural, demonic. For where jealousy and selfish ambition exist, there is disorder and every evil thing. But the wisdom from above is first pure, then peaceable, gentle, reasonable, full of mercy and good fruits, unwavering, without hypocrisy.

"But wisdom from above is...*without hypocrisy.*" Heavenly wisdom must be characterized by integrity—with purity of motive and wholeness of character. But where hypocrisy is present, heavenly wisdom is absent. Wisdom may be present, but it is wisdom from below—earthly, demonic wisdom. The wisdom, or skill, that a Christian exhibits in decision-making and interactions with individuals cannot afford to be accompanied by ulterior motives or inconsistencies between what is said or presented and what is actually done. Even in the church, there are far too many instances where individuals are counseled to compromise truthfulness or honesty in order to attain a desired outcome or achieve a particular goal.

I myself can recall a number of instances when I was counseled or encouraged by an older saint in the church to pretend that I was in agreement with another person with whom I was not in actual agreement. I was once even told that I should simply "play the game" in order to win people to myself. In effect, I was told to be a hypocrite so that I could win a particular person to myself.

But such a sentiment doesn't just exist in the realm of personal relationships; it exists in the corporate realm as well. I was once in a training session at a company where I was newly hired as a sales agent. During one of our sessions, our lecturer said that one of key qualities of a good salesman is "making believe that they need the product even if, in reality, they don't need it." In other words, the way to make money is to twist people into believing something that you know isn't true—all in the name of skill. In other words, compromise truth for material gain at the expense of people's money. Needless to say, I quit the job during that week of training, and the Lord graciously provided me with another job very shortly after.

There is a difference between heavenly wisdom and worldly cunning. Worldly cunning is crafty, manipulative, deceitful and compromises virtue in order to gain either the goods of the world or the following of people. Worldly cunning knows how to manipulate and deceive individuals for the desired gain—be it wealth, power, popularity, or whatever else. Thus, when integrity is absent and virtue is compromised, whatever craft is exhibited is not true wisdom, nor is it pleasing to God. Heavenly wisdom must always be free of hypocrisy and full of integrity.

Where Hypocrisy is Present, Godly Prayer is Absent

Every Christian is called to pray. Prayer is one of the greatest privileges that God has given us. We are the only creatures endowed with the ability to consciously and worshipfully talk to God. That said, just because one prays doesn't mean God is pleased. Not surprisingly, Jesus not only encourages us to pray, he also instructs us how and how *not* to pray.

> When you pray, you are not to be like the hypocrites; for they love to stand and pray in the synagogues and on the street corners so that they may be seen by men. Truly I say to you, they have their reward in full. But you, when you pray, go into your inner room, close your door and pray to your Father who is in secret, and your Father who sees what is done in secret will reward you (Matt 6:5-6).

Christ's first instruction on how not to pray is this: *when you pray, don't pray hypocritically*. Godly prayer and hypocrisy cannot coexist. They are mutually exclusive, and the presence of one implies the absence of the other. It is not simply the act of praying, then, that brings pleasure to God from the believer, but also the manner and motivation by which those prayers are lifted. Specifically, those who claim to belong to Christ ought be cautious lest their prayers are characterized by hypocrisy.

Christ vividly describes how hypocrites pray in verse 5. First, their prayers are made almost exclusively in public. Second, they pray to be seen, noticed, and gain the esteem of others. It was the motivation, more than the method, that Jesus condemns. There is nothing inherently sinful about praying on the street or in a synagogue. After all, God commands us to love Him and speak of Him whether we are sitting in our homes, walking on the road, lying down, or rising up (Deut 6:7). And there is obviously nothing wrong with public prayer, as God actually commands it (1 Tim 2:1-8). But the hypocritical Pharisees who Jesus exposed didn't pray out of a reverence for God. Prayers were designed by God to be an act of worship, and the act that gives praise to God. The Pharisees engaged in an act that pretended to give glory to God in order to receive glory from men. Their prayers were performances. Thus, Jesus says about their prayers, "Truly I say to you, they have their reward in full" (Matt 6:1 In other words, all the hypocrites will enjoy is the fleeting praise of men. God will turn away from the prayers of a hypocrite because they are an abomination to Him.

I've often joked that people frequently use the line, "I'll be praying for you" as a way to end a conversation that they don't want to be in. There is, however, some truth to this joke: people often employ prayer to disguise another reality. In other words, it is not uncommon for someone to pray publicly for something that they honestly don't care about and, in their hearts, don't really care to ask God about.

I know this not because I can read people's hearts, but because Christ Himself in Matthew 6 exposed this reality about people. One way to know that your prayers are marked by hypocrisy is if the manner and content of your prayers in public are never repeated genuinely in private before God. A prayer life that is pleasing to God, as Christ instructs, has a private element to it: "But you, when you pray, go into your inner room, close your door, and pray to your Father who is in secret, and your Father who sees what is done in secret will reward you" (Matt 6:6). Hypocrites don't have a vibrant private prayer life because they have no real relationship with God such that they would actually want to pray to Him when He is the only one in the audience.

As Christians, we must be careful to employ prayer for one purpose and one purpose only—to speak to God out of a worshipful love for Him. We must be wary of ever using prayer for the sake of gaining information from others for the sake of gossip. We must be cautious of using prayer as a means to impress people and make them think highly of our own outward spirituality. To have integrity in prayer means to pray for no other purpose than to truly talk to God, either for Him to move His hand upon a request we are making or to praise Him for things that He has done or is doing. When such motive is absent, prayers become hypocritical. And when they become hypocritical, they are better off not spoken, because God will not listen to them.

Where Hypocrisy is Present, Intake of the Word of God is Absent

Every Christian is called to regularly take in the Word of God. Along with prayer, reading Scripture is the most vital discipline for the Christian. A Christian without the Word of God is as dangerously famished as an infant without milk. For this reason, Peter instructs Christians in 1 Peter 2:2: "like newborn babies, long for the pure milk of the word, so that by it you may grow in respect to salvation." It is only when one continually receives the Word of God into his heart and mind that he will actually grow toward maturity and completion in Christ (Col 1:28).

This instruction is true for both laymen and leaders. Concerning the latter, Paul reminds Timothy that a pastor is to be "constantly nourished in the words of the faith and of sound doctrine" in order to be a good servant of Christ Jesus (1 Tim 4:6) and later reminds Timothy himself that it was the Scriptures that are "able go give you the wisdom that leads to salvation through faith which is in Christ Jesus" (2 Tim 3:15). However, just because one reads or hears the Word of God regularly—either through his own personal Bible reading times or through listening to sermons preached—does not necessarily mean that he is truly receiving it as God intended. Thus, before Peter instructs Christians to long for the Scriptures in 1 Peter 2:2, he gives the condition by which a person must do so in verse 2:1: "Therefore, putting aside all malice and all deceit and *hypocrisy* and envy and all slander." In order for one to truly receive the Word of God in the manner that God intended, one must first put off hypocrisy. Thus, where hypocrisy is present, the true intake of the Word of God is not. A hypocrite, in other words, can read and hear the Word but he cannot truly receive it.

As a young Christian, I had been encouraged by several older Christians to regularly have what is commonly referred to in Christian circles as a "quiet time." It's sometimes called "doing your devotions." These are colloquial terms that refer to the daily reading of Scripture. For this reason, many Christians will share about how consistent they are in daily reading their Bibles when asked about how they are doing spiritually. For the record, there is nothing wrong with Christians implementing quiet times into their lives. It is indeed a very helpful spiritual discipline. But it must be remembered that the New Testament doesn't command us to physically and privately read our

English Bibles everyday (though again, such a practice can be helpful). What it does command us is to hear the Word and do it effectually. To read the Word regularly without actually obeying it—or making any sustained effort to do so—is pointless. The man who does this is deluded (James 1:22). More than that, he is a hypocrite. Unfortunately, such people exist in the church. There are professing Christians whom I have heard boast about how consistently they read and study their Bibles whose lives are completely antithetical to the Scriptures and yet make excuses when their disobedience and hypocrisy is confronted. Their lives remain stunted, showing very few—if any—signs of true growth. And the reason? Because for all the reading and hearing and studying of the Word that they claim to do, they never truly received it, as they had failed to put aside their hypocrisy. How vital, then, it is for us to exhibit integrity in our lives and motives whenever we approach the Word of God.

Where Hypocrisy is Present, True teaching of the Word of God is Absent

There is no more vital and pivotal ministry in the church than the preaching and teaching of God's Word. The importance of biblical instruction cannot be overemphasized. It was when the teaching of the Word was absent that Israel began to drift away into idolatry and eventually fall into captivity. It was with the teaching of the Word by Ezra that God's people were reformed and rebuilt. It was through the proclamation of Christ and the teaching of His Word that the early church grew. And it is through the faithful preaching and teaching of God's Word by those whom He has gifted to preach and teach that the church continues to grow today.

However, not everyone who claims to be a teacher of God's Word is worthy to be listened to or followed. In the visible church, mixed with—and often, at first glance, indistinguishable from—the shepherds are wolves. Alongside true teachers of the Word exist false teachers who pretend to teach the Word. What characterizes these teachers? No surprise, false teachers can be identified by their hypocrisy. Paul warned Timothy about these teachers and instructed Timothy to silence them in Ephesus.

> But the Spirit explicitly says that in later times some will fall away from the faith, saying attention to deceitful spirits and doctrines of demons, by means of the *hypocrisy* of liars seared in their own conscience as with a branding iron, men who forbid marriage and advocate abstaining from foods which God has created to be gratefully shared in by those who believe and know the truth (1 Tim 4:1-3).

How is it that people in the visible church will fall away from the faith? By paying attention to deceitful spirits and doctrines of demons. And who is responsible for teaching such things? False teachers—liars, as Paul calls them. And by what are these false teachers characterized? Hypocrisy. False teachers, in other words, will deceive others into falling away from the faith by the means of their own hypocrisy. Hypocrisy is as dangerous as it is detestable. It is detestable because God hates it; it is dangerous because of the influence it can have on otherwise innocent people. Thus, where hypocrisy is present, the true teaching of the Word of God is compromised.

For the record, those who minister as preachers and teachers will not be perfect in this lifetime, nor should we expect them to be. But true ministers of the Word are also characterized by integrity. God designed for His Word to be taught by people, and such people are marked by integrity. When we evaluate a preacher and teacher, it is not only important to discern sound doctrine from heretical doctrine; it is equally important to discern integrity from hypocrisy regarding the character of the Bible teacher.

This recognition of a teacher's character is vital because a hypocrite—no matter how theologically astute or conservative he may be—will inevitably lead those under him into error, deception, and stumbling. It is for this reason that the author of Hebrews exhorts Christians to consider the outcome of the lives of those who speak the Word of God (Heb 13:7). In order for the man of God to truly teach the Word of God the way

God designed for His Word to be instructed, his character, though not perfect, must be free from hypocrisy. It is for this reason that the first moral qualification for elders is that he be "above reproach" (1 Tim 3:2), for when there is hypocrisy in the teacher, there is deception in his teaching. And when there is deception in the teaching, there is potential for people to be led astray. No matter how many degrees a man earns from renowned Bible seminaries and institutions, he will not be able to adequately teach people God's Word in a way that leads them to completeness in Christ if his character is marred by hypocrisy.

Where Hypocrisy is Present, Godly Ministry and Service is Absent

All Christians are called to fulfill their ministry to the church and serve the Lord. It should never be the case where eighty percent of the work in the church is carried out by twenty percent of the people. Pastors and teachers are not responsible to carry the entire ministry of the church on their shoulders; rather, they are to equip all the saints to do the work of ministry (Eph 4:12). Each believer—whether he is a vocational leader or a layman—has been entrusted by God with a spiritual gift and is responsible to employ this gift for the glory of God (1 Pet 4:10-11) and the edification of the body of Christ (1 Cor 12:7, 14:12; Eph 4:13-16).

However, as with all other duties in Christian living, ministering and serving in the church must also be done in the right manner. Just because one is serving or ministering in the church does not automatically mean that God is pleased with what he is doing. It is not only the action of serving that matters, but also the character behind the service. And as with all other Christian duties, ministry and service will only be pleasing to God when it is free from hypocrisy. Jesus warns against hypocritical serving and ministry in Matthew 6:2-4:

> So when you give to the poor, do not sound a trumpet before you, as the *hypocrites* do in the synagogues and in the streets, so that they may be honored by men. Truly I say to you, they have their reward in full. But when you give to the poor, do not let your left hand know what your right hand is doing, so that your giving will be in secret; and your Father who sees what is done in secret will reward you.

Giving to the poor in this passage represents a broader category of good deeds including humanitarian service and other noble things that we do for others. This could be informal deeds that we do for others, such as helping an elderly lady cross the street, or formal ministries that we do in the church. How, then, are we supposed to engage in ministry and good deeds? Christ is clear: we are to serve in a way that is not like the hypocrites. Christ's condemned the Pharisees, not for the act of giving to the poor, but for how they purposefully drew attention to themselves in order to gain the honor and esteem of men. What was meant to be a deed done for others (giving to the poor) was motivated by a desire for self-glory (that they may be honored by men). The Pharisees' external deeds were incompatible with their internal desires; they were hypocrites. Christ says that, because of this, "they have their reward in full." In other words, they would not be rewarded by God, as God is not pleased with their deeds. For where hypocrisy is present, godly ministry and service is absent.

In other words, it's not just about what you do but also why you do it. Now you may say, "I can't remember the last time I actually took out a brass trumpet and blew it after I did something good for someone." But before you let yourself off the hook, let me ask you, When was the last time you created a Facebook post about something good that you did, hoping that you'd get your fifty "likes" and comments from others saying what a wonderful person you are? Let me ask you, When was the last time you told people you were "tired," not because you really were tired, but because you wanted them to ask you why it is that you were tired…so that you could have an opportunity tell them all of the good deeds that you've been doing? Are you someone who craves for attention and keeps track of what you do in order to put it on public display? If so, you are ministering as a hypocrite would, and God Himself will withhold rewards from you.

We live in a culture that is obsessed with displaying our deeds and publicizing our piety, so serving with integrity will be like swimming upstream. Our culture is obsessed with resumés that embellish our credentials, social media that displays our deeds, and titles that communicate our accomplishments. As Christians, we must swim against that current, no matter how difficult it is. For once we begin to do what we do for publicity and honor, we have fallen into hypocrisy.

Where Hypocrisy is Present, Proper Confrontation of Sin is Absent

Confrontation of sin is absolutely vital in the church. Where there is no confrontation, sin in the body will not be dealt with as God intends. Contrary to how some have twisted Scripture, the Bible does indeed say to judge and to do so righteously (John 7:24). As Christians, we are called to confront the sins of one another (Matt 18:15) and deal with them accordingly. However, there is a proper way to confront sin, and there is an improper way. The proper way is marked by humility; the improper, by hypocrisy. Regarding confrontation of sin amongst believers, Christ instructs his disciples:

> Why do you look at the speck that is in your brother's eye, but do not notice the log that is in your own eye? Or how can you say to your brother, 'Let me take the speck out of your eye,' and behold, the log is in your eye?

> You *hypocrite*, first take the log out of your
> own eye, and then you will see clearly to take
> the speck out of your brother's eye (Matt 7:3-
> 5).

Hypocrites, according to Jesus, are not only experts in tooting their horn when doing good deeds, but also in pointing out others' sinful deeds. Confrontation of sin becomes improper and inappropriate when the confronter points out the speck in the eyes of the other while failing to first take out the log in his own eye. While confrontation of others' sins is warranted in the church, self-confrontation is a priority. When the latter is not practiced, hypocrisy will be exhibited.

For the record, Jesus is not commanding us to abstain from confronting sin. Rather, He instructs us to confront sin properly and in a godly manner. It is important for Christians, when considering how to confront the sins of another, to first ask if they are in the proper position to confront the sin.

During my years as a school teacher, I can recall several instances when a fellow colleague would take it upon himself or herself to admonish me for a particular issue—whether it was related to my teaching style, room upkeep, classroom management, or others. Over time, I learned to ignore them. It wasn't out of arrogance; it was due to the realization that the things they were admonishing me about were issues about which they themselves were being admonished by higher administration. I would scratch my head at why colleagues would go out of their way to help someone in an area in which they themselves were deficient. To this day, I still wonder why she walked into my room that day. At the same time, it doesn't take rocket science to figure out that the people who are often the most critical of others are also the people whose lives are a mess. How unfitting it is for you to try to take out the speck from your brother's eye when you have a forest in yours! To confront sin hypocritically is to confront sin unbiblically

Where Hypocrisy is Present,
True Humility is Absent

There is no question that humility before God and others is absolutely vital to Christian character. God is opposed to the proud but gives grace to the humble (James 4:6; 1 Pet 5:5). God Himself says that His eyes, though they see all of His creation, look especially upon those who humble themselves before Him (Isa 66:2). However, humility can only be truly exhibited when hypocrisy is absent. Otherwise, whatever act of humility done will be disregarded by God. Christ shows us this in Matthew 6:16: "Whenever you fast, do not put on a gloomy face as the *hypocrites* do, for they neglect their appearance so that they will be noticed by men when they are fasting. Truly I say to you, they have their reward in full."

Back in biblical times, fasting was an act that was meant to display humility. Ezra the scribe, in his journey from Babylon to Jerusalem, proclaimed a fast at the river of Ahava amongst all the Jews with whom he was traveling "that we might *humble* ourselves before our God to seek from Him a safe journey for us, our little ones, and all our possessions" (Ezra 8:21). But, according to Christ's words, acts associated with humility are only regarded favorably by God when they are done in a way that is distinct from how the hypocrites conduct themselves. When the hypocritical Pharisees fasted they would purposefully make themselves look ugly and dirty and disheveled, wear ragged clothes, and even dump ash on themselves. They wanted to look gloomy in order for people to think that they were pious. Though they did acts that were often associated with humility, they themselves were not considered humble by God because of their hypocrisy. Again, there was an incongruity between what they were presenting to people and the true ambition behind their actions. It was the presence of their hypocrisy that revealed the total absence of actual humility.

It must be noted that acts of self-deprecation often associated with humility can be just as prideful as self-promotion, when done out of the ambition to draw attention. While we ought to be honest about our sins and shortcomings to one another (James 5:16), we have to be careful not to do so with a motivation to earn the praise of others. If you tell others how bad you are because you want them to tell you how good you are, then you obviously don't think you're that bad! Often times, those who have a habit of publicly putting themselves down are also those who are hungry for attention and praise. Such self-deprecation is not humility. It is hypocrisy—pretending to hate your sin while in reality being in love with attention. A truly humble person doesn't seek to draw attention to himself, either by self-promotion or self-deprecation, because he desires God to be the sole recipient of people's praise (Matt 5:16).

Where Hypocrisy is Present, True Love is Absent

Without love, one cannot truly claim to be of God. Those who are born of God will love (1 John 4:7), for God is love (1 John 4:8). And yet love divorced from integrity is not the kind of love that God commands from His children. In Romans 12:9, Paul commands Christians: "let love be without *hypocrisy*. Abhor what is evil; cling to what is good." Love must be free from ulterior motives. Love must be free from hidden agendas. Acts that are associated with love are not love if accompanied by the wrong motivation. To say that you love someone because of the attention, affection, appreciation or adulation that you receive from them is not love; it is lust, even if it is non-sexual. This is why hypocrisy is so dangerous; its presence indicates that whatever acts of love we claim to do are not true love.

And when we are not truly loving, we are not behaving in a manner consistent with those born of God.

Love also must be free from empty words and free from inconsistency between words and actions, or actions and motives. The apostle John explains this further in 1 John 3:16-18:

> We know love by this, that He laid down His life for us; and we ought to lay down our lives for the brethren. But whoever has the world's goods, and sees his brother in need and closes his heart against him, how does the love of God abides him? Little children, let us not love with word or with tongue, but in deed and truth.

Genuine love needs no verbal defense. If you truly love another person in the way that Christ loved us, you would not have to say things like, "You know that I did this because I love you." There are, for instance, a number of people in my life who have never actually verbalized the words "I love you" to me. And yet, without a shadow of a doubt, I can affirm that they are the ones that love me and my family the most. Why? Because it is during those times when we were in greatest need that they were there to support us, carry our burdens, and meet those needs while sacrificing their own. Love is not something that is carried out primarily by tongue, but by deed. Love is proven not by the verbal statement "I love you," but by the act of self-sacrifice for the welfare of another. When such actions are absent, John's rhetorical question is, "How does the love of God abide in him?" In other words, where hypocrisy is present, the love of God is absent.

Where Hypocrisy is Present, Acceptable Worship is Absent

Humans were created to worship God. It is the first commandment for a reason (Exod 20:1-6). A Christian is someone who has turned away from false worship and worships the true and only living God (1 Thess 1:9). The one in whom worship of God is absent is the one in whom the Christian faith is absent. And yet, just because one engages in traditional acts associated with worship—be it liturgical or musical—does not mean that his worship is acceptable or pleasing to God. Christ describes such vain worship when exposing the Pharisees in Mark 7:6-7:

> Rightly did Isaiah prophesy of you *hypocrites*, as it is written: "This people honors Me with their lips, but their heart is far from Me. But in vain do they worship Me, teaching as doctrines the precepts of men."

What is it that made the worship of the Pharisees and religious leaders vain? It wasn't because they weren't singing long enough. It wasn't because they didn't wear the right ceremonial attire. It wasn't because they messed up on their recitations. It wasn't because their theological knowledge was incorrect. It was because they were hypocrites. For where hypocrisy is present, acceptable and substantial worship is absent. The two are mutually exclusive.

Before explaining this further, it must be noted that as Christians we will never be perfect—either in action, motive, will, or desire. If we expect ourselves to be perfect before we attend a Sunday worship service, then we'll never be able to go. Again, perfection and integrity are not synonymous. What Christ is condemning here in the Pharisees is a blatant disconnect between what they say and where their heart truly is at. All the things done that are typically associated with worship—from praying to singing to reading Scripture to whatever else—are utter vanity when performed by a person whose heart is far from God.

Where Hypocrisy is Present,
Christian Living is Absent

What then does a person who exhibits deep, unrepentant hypocrisy have left? The Scriptures are clear about what he lacks. He is void of heavenly wisdom, true humility, and true love, which makes him void of Christian character. He is without acceptable worship, prayer, and the true intake of God's Word, making him void of Christian disciplines. He is void of true ministry and proper confrontation of sin, making Him void of Christian responsibilities. Where hypocrisy is present, therefore, Christian living is absent. And where Christian living is absent, Christianity is absent. Hypocrisy, then, is no small issue. To the life of a professing Christian, it is a destructive wild fire that rips through every aspect of a person's life. Therefore, every Christian must be aware of its presence in his or her life and squelch it immediately—however small it may be at the time. Otherwise, if left unchecked, it will eventually grow and destroy every aspect of the Christian's life.

Conclusion

The Gospel and Freedom from Hypocrisy

Everyone, to some degree, will struggle with hypocrisy. It was at a Shepherds Conference in Southern California where one of the keynote speakers once said, "It's not a matter of whether or not you struggle with hypocrisy; it's how much of it you exhibit." It is possible for a Christian to struggle with being selfishly competitive. It is possible for a growing believer to still struggle with remnants of legalism. It is definitely possible for a Christian to struggle with moral inconsistencies. It is possible for Christians to fall into moral disproportion. Every Christian I know has admitted to struggling with ulterior motives. It is possible for a truly regenerate individual to struggle with pretense. Every regenerate Christian is still prone to falling into hypocrisy in some way. Hypocrisy is not necessarily a sign that a person is an unbeliever.

This truth can be illustrated by considering the lives of two of the early church's leading Christians, the apostle Peter and Barnabas. Both stumbled into hypocrisy and were confronted by the apostle Paul. The incident is recorded in summary form in Galatians 2:11-14. The event of their stumbling occurred in early in the life of the church shortly after the initial inclusion of the Gentiles into the body of Christ. When the apostle Peter visited the church in Antioch—a local congregation that consisted of both Jewish and Gentile Christians—he extended fellowship with both groups. Jewish by culture, Peter understood the universal reach of the gospel to all people groups and he was more than willing to share meals with his Gentile brothers and sisters. Thus, he "used to eat with the Gentiles" (Gal 2:12).

This period, however, was also marked by the increasing presence of Judaizing legalism in the early church, a movement that arose as a reaction by some Jews to the fact that Gentile Christians were not being circumcised upon salvation. These legalists were also referred to as the party of the circumcision, specifically because they insisted that Gentile converts to Christianity were obligated to obey the Jewish ceremonial law of circumcision. As a result, division and segregation began to infiltrate the Antioch church, specifically with Jewish legalists within the church purposefully and unduly excluding Gentiles from fellowship. As the leading apostle in the early church (Acts 2), the Jewish legalists began to put pressure on Peter to withhold fellowship from the Gentiles when they arrived in Antioch. Galatians 2:14 summarizes Peter's reaction to their arrival: "he began to withdraw and hold himself aloof, fearing the party of the circumcision."

Though he was one of the leading ministers of the gospel who preached justification by faith apart from the works of the Law, Peter began to withhold fellowship from Gentile Christians, fellow recipients of the gospel, because of their lack of adherence to the works of the Law. The content of his preaching was betrayed by the course of his actions. Paul records the resulting impact of Peter's actions: "The rest of the Jews joined him in *hypocrisy*, with the result that even Barnabas was carried away by their *hypocrisy*" (Gal 2:13). Even Barnabas, the son of encouragement who preached the gospel to the Gentiles alongside Paul in the first missionary journey was carried away by Peter's actions. Paul referred to this incongruity between the gospel they preached and the way the conducted themselves as hypocrisy. Indeed, both Peter and Barnabas (along with other Jewish Christians) were guilty of hypocrisy.

Yet there is a massive difference between stumbling into hypocrisy and being characterized by hypocrisy. Though they stumbled into hypocrisy, Peter and Barnabas were no doubt genuine Christians, true leaders of the church, and destined for heaven. They may have fallen into *hypocrisy*, but they were not *hypocrites*.

So how can you determine if you are a hypocrite? The solution is simple: evaluate whether all seven of the signs of hypocrisy that Christ speaks of appear in you comprehensively, continually, and consistently. Allow me to turn to the world of dogs as an example.

There are many dogs that weigh about 130 pounds. There are many dogs that stand about 30 inches to the withers (the highest part of the back). There are many dogs with long, thin muzzles. There are many dogs with upright, pointed ears. There are many dogs that have grizzled gray and white fur. There are many dogs that have long, slender legs and narrow chests. There are many dogs with powerful jaws. There are many dogs with a strong hunting instinct. It is possible for a domestic dog to exhibit any one, or two, of these characteristics. But if a Siberian Husky breeder tries to sell me one of his dogs that weighs 130 pounds, stands 30 inches to the withers, has a long and thin muzzle, has upright and pointed ears, has grizzled gray and white fur, has long slender legs and a narrow chest, has powerful jaws, and has a strong hunting instinct...I would look him straight in the eye and say, "Sir, that's no dog you have. That's a wolf!"

If those closest to you say you are selfishly competitive, cultural legalistic, morally inconsistent, morally disproportionate, wrongly motivated, pretentiously unwholesome, and self-righteous, then there is good reason to question the condition of your faith. Here's why: to the Pharisees and scribes who did exhibit all seven signs, Jesus said, "How will you escape the sentence of hell?" In other words, the Pharisees and scribes were not believers who struggled with hypocrisy; they were not believers at all. They were unregenerate pretenders who were headed to hell. A hypocritical faith, if it stays hypocritical, will not save. If you, then, are currently wearing a mask of Christianity, then take it off. Because if you don't, God will eventually take it off for you. Oh how tragic if the first thing you hear from Jesus on the Day of Judgment is this: "You're a fake! Your whole life was an act!" Woe to the man who enters eternity and receives an Oscar and not a crown.

The Gospel and a Life Free of Hypocrisy

What is the solution to hypocrisy? What is the foundation for integrity in the Christian? It is none other than the gospel of Jesus Christ. As mentioned earlier, hypocrisy is first and foremost a condition of the heart. The only way to live with integrity, therefore, is to have a transformed heart. Jesus Himself says, "Blessed are the pure at heart, for they shall see God" (Matt 5:8). How wonderful it is to know that our Great Physician is a spiritual cardiologist. The gospel of Jesus Christ is not merely declarative; it is transformative. All those who believe in Him are given new hearts (Ezek

36:26). A heart impacted by the gospel produces a life of integrity.

The man who knows Christ as Lord and Savior won't try to look pretty on the outside; rather, he looks to God to save him from his sins (Rom 7:24-8:1). Such a man won't ever pretend to have it all together, because he knows that his sin is what put Christ on the cross (1 Tim 1:12-17). He won't panic when people realize that he's a sinner, because he knows that Christ paid the full price for his sins. He won't care about how others think of him, because he knows that Christ is taking him to heaven (Luke 10:20). He won't care whether or not he wins an Oscar, because he knows that reserved for him in heaven is the crown of life (2 Tim 4:6-8). The person who is transformed by the gospel is the person in whom hypocrisy is being mortified and in whom integrity is pervasive.

Integrity is not an impossible quality to attain. It is not only commanded to us by God; it is expected of us. And it is not only expected of us; it is needed from us. The church has been polluted by hypocrisy since its dawning (1 Tim 4:2), and it constantly gasps for the purified air that can only flow from those men and women with such wholesome Christian character. Where, then, are the men and women of integrity? Where are the ministers of God who, like the apostle Paul, can testify with a clear conscience that they have conducted themselves in holiness and godly sincerity (2

Cor 1:12)? It is my hope that you, whoever you are reading this book, are one of those people.

ABOUT THE AUTHOR

J.R. Cuevas graduated from The Master's Seminary and currently pastors at Creekside Bible Church in Cupertino, California. J. R. lives with his wife and two children in San Jose, California, where he also serves as a Bible teacher at a local Christian school.

ABOUT WITH ALL WISDOM

With All Wisdom is the Christian media creation ministry located in Cupertino, CA. We started this publishing ministry out of the simple desire to serve the local body with substantive biblical resources for the sake of our people's growth and spiritual maturity.

But we also believe that book publishing, like any other Christian ministry, should first and foremost be under the supervision and accountability of the local church. While we are grateful for and will continue to support the many excellent traditional publishers available today—our shelves are full of the books they have produced—we also believe that the best place to develop solid, life-giving theology and biblical instruction is within the local church.

With All Wisdom is also unique because we offer our books at a very low cost. We strive for excellence in our writing and seek to provide a high-quality product to our readers. Our editorial team is comprised of men and women who are highly trained and excellent in their craft. But since we are able to avoid the high overhead costs that are typically incurred by traditional publishers, we are able to pass significant savings on to you. The result is a growing collection of books that are substantive, readable, and affordable.

In order to best serve various spiritual and theological needs of the body of Christ, we have developed three distinct lines of books. **Big Truth | little books®** provides readers with accessible, manageable works on theology, Christian living, and important church and social issues in a format that is easy to read and easy to finish. Our **Equip Series** is aimed at Christians who desire to delve a little deeper into doctrine and practical matters of the faith. Our **Foundations Series** is our academic line in which we seek to contribute to the contemporary theological discussion by combining pastoral perspective with rigorous scholarship.

OTHER TITLES FROM WITH ALL WISDOM PUBLICATIONS

Please visit us at WithAllWisdom.org
to learn more about these titles

BIG TRUTH little books®
A Biblical View of Trials
Cliff McManis

What the Bible Says About Gray Areas
Cliff McManis

Faith: The Gift of God
Cliff McManis

How to Pray for Your Pastor
Derek Brown

The Problem of Evil
Cliff McManis

What the Bible Says About Government
Cliff McManis

God Defines and Defends Marriage
Cliff McManis

*Protecting the Flock: The Priority of
Church Membership*
Cliff McManis

What the Bible Says About Confrontation
Cliff McManis

*Fellowship with God: A Guide to Bible Reading,
Meditation, and Prayer*
Derek Brown

What the Bible Says About Hospitality
Cliff McManis

The Danger of Hypocrisy
J. R. Cuevas

Equip
*The Biblically-Driven Church:
How Jesus Builds His Body*
Cliff McManis

*God's Glorious Story:
The Truth of What It's All About*
Colin Eakin

*Strong and Courageous: The Character and Calling of
Mature Manhood*
Derek Brown

The Gospel, the Church, and Homosexuality: How the Gospel is Still the Power of God for Redemption and Transformation
Edited by Michael Sanelli and Derek Brown

Foundations
Apologetics by the Book
Cliff McManis

www.ingramcontent.com/pod-product-compliance
Lightning Source LLC
Chambersburg PA
CBHW020509030426
42337CB00011B/304